T0055804

**Tobias Picker**
b.1954

# Dove Aria

from *Thérèse Raquin*
for Mezzo-Soprano and Piano

Libretto by Gene Scheer
Based on the novel by Emile Zola

ED 30093

www.schott-music.com

Mainz · London · Madrid · New York · Paris · Prague · Tokyo · Toronto
© 2000 SCHOTT HELICON MUSIC CORPORATION, New York · Printed in USA

# Dove Aria

from "Thérèse Raquin"

Gene Scheer

Tobias Picker

Lyrics: The white dove sat in the cor-ner of the ark for for-ty days and for-ty nights. Her ti-ny feath-ers trem—

ED30093

- - - 'bling in the dark,_____ her small head bu-ried_____ in ter-ror_____ and fright.

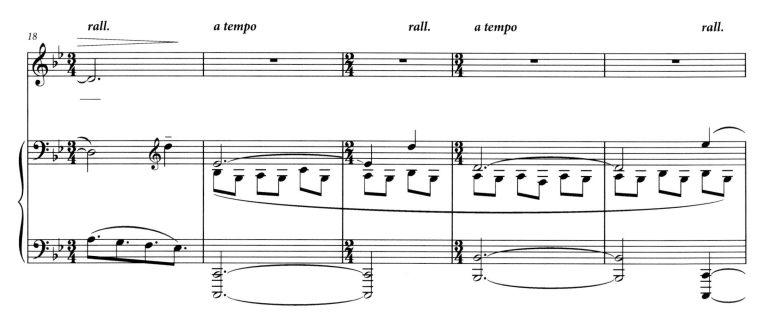

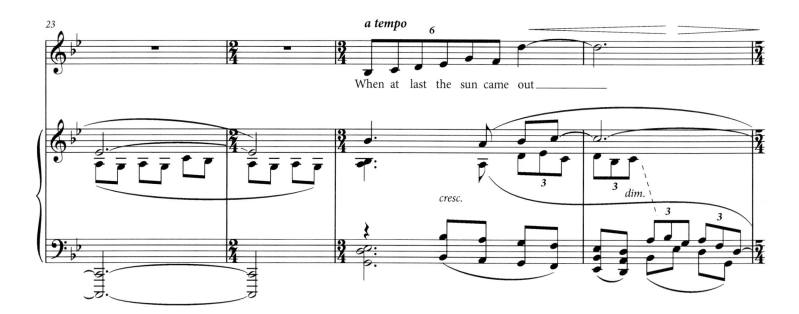

When at last the sun came out_____

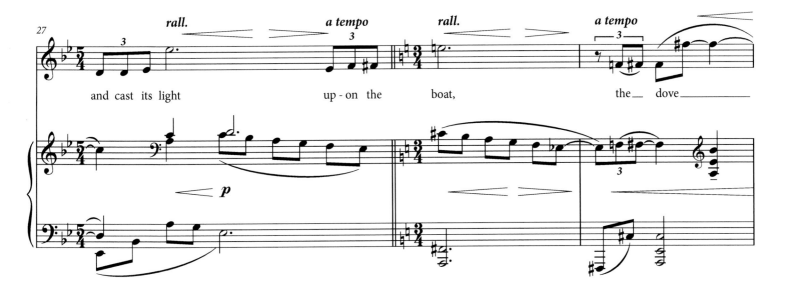

and cast its light up - on the boat, the dove___

took wing and all could see

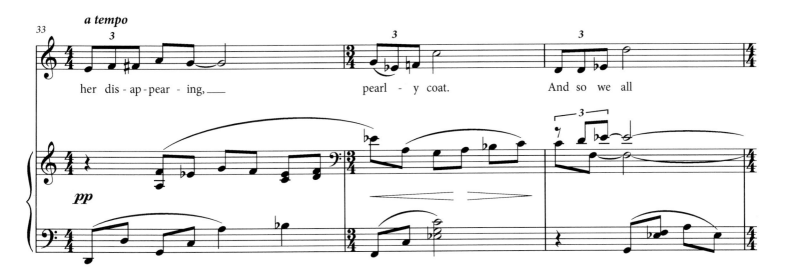

her dis - ap - pear - ing,___ pearl - y coat. And so we all

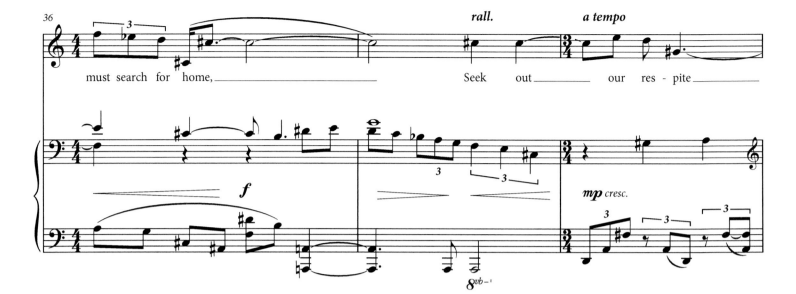

and soothe the ter - rors of the night,

just as the gen - - - - - - - - - tle, faith - ful dove.

*rall.* *a tempo*

Un poco meno tranquillo ♩ = 54

Who will take me to

*pp sub.*

firm land? Who_____ can lead me to a place of rest?

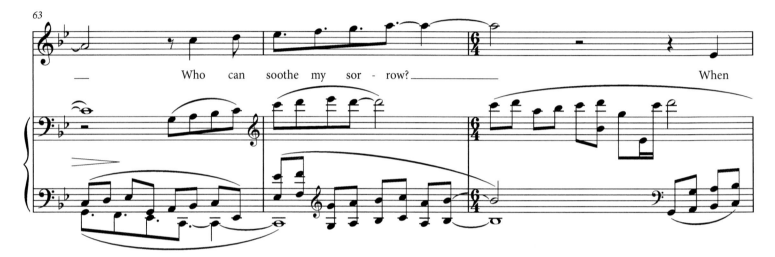

Who can soothe my sor - row?_____ When

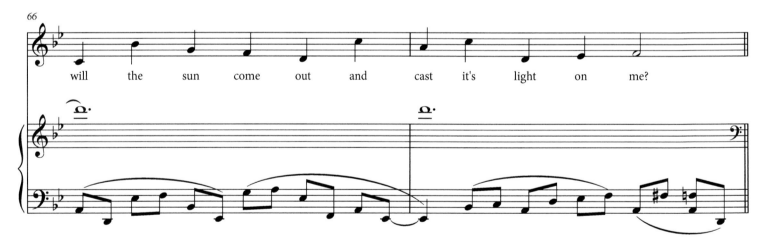

will the sun come out and cast it's light on me?

What can end my sor-row? Where is_____ my faith - ful dove?_____

**Schott Helicon Music Corporation**

254 West 31st Street, 15th Floor
New York, NY 10001
Tel: 212 461 6940
Fax: 212 810 4565
ny@schott-music.com

ISBN-13: 978-1-4803-4443-3

Distributed By

HAL LEONARD

49019581

HL 49019581
ISBN: 978-1-48034-443-3

DISTRIBUTED IN NORTH AND SOUTH AMERICA
EXCLUSIVELY BY

HAL LEONARD
CORPORATION
49019581